On The Edge Of The Knife

On The Edge Of The Knife

by Charles Edward Eaton

The Abelard Poets

ABELARD-SCHUMAN
LONDON   NEW YORK   TORONTO

811.54
Ea 80

74730
July, 1971

LONDON   NEW YORK   TORONTO
Abelard-Schuman   Abelard-Schuman   Abelard-Schuman
Limited   Limited   Canada Limited
8 King St. WC 2   257 Park Ave. So.   1680 Midland Ave.

An Intext Publisher

Printed in the United States of America

ACKNOWLEDGMENTS

The Reporter first published "The Parrot," "The Parure," "Chores," "The Last Page But One," "The Turkey," and "The Clown."

The Sewanee Review first published "The Savage," "The Possible Dreams of Swans," and "Sun Figure."

The Hollins Critic first published "Schooling the Walrus," "The Camel," and "The Museum."

Quarterly Review of Literature first published "On the Fringe," "The Gallery," "The Midget," and "In the Hammock."

The Virginia Quarterly Review first published "The Shopping Center."

Acknowledgments are also due to the following magazines for permission to reprint one or more poems: *The Saturday Review, The Chicago Review, Commonweal, Epoch, University* (Princeton), *Beloit Poetry Journal, Perspective, Trace, The University Review* (Kansas City), *Sparrow Magazine, Southern Poetry Review, Chelsea Review, Northwest Review, Four Quarters, The Literary Review, Impetus, Poetry Northwest, Lillabulero, Yale Literary Magazine, The Mad River Review, American Weave, Prism International* (Canada), *The Cambridge Review* (England), *Delta,* (Cambridge, England), *The Dublin Review* (Ireland), *The Lugano Review* (Switzerland), and *Meanjin* (Australia).

Also, "Some, Not All," first published in *Northwest Review,* was anthologized in BEST POEMS OF 1962, and "The Tree-Frog," first published in *The Saturday Review,* was included in BEST POEMS OF 1965 (Pacific Books). "The Siamese Twins" was anthologized in RED CLAY READER, 1967. "The Gondola" was included in the anthology of American poetry in translation published by *Editions de la Revue Moderne* (Paris). "The Goose," first published in *Poetry Northwest,* was included in BEST POEMS OF 1968 (Pacific Books). "The Fish Observed," first published in *Western Humanities Review,* was anthologized in EAST OF AMERICA (Chatham Press), 1969.

CONTENTS

I

The Parrot
The Shopping Center
The Parure
Chores
The Tree-Frog
With the Shock Troops
Rebuttal
The Last Page But One

II

On the Edge of the Knife
Some, Not All
The Savage
The Lepidopterist
On the Fringe
October
The Turkey

III

The Fish Observed
Skin Diver
The Beach
The Consul
The Vendetta
Voyeur
The Lobster
Pool at Night

IV

Schooling the Walrus
The Mistress
The Siamese Twins
The Bird Fan Woman's As If
Watermelon
The Mulatto
Inventory at an Autumn Window

V

The Possible Dreams of Swans
The Clown
The Gallery
The Goose
The Midget
The Giggler
Skin Tales
The Impersonator

VI

The Camel
Bird Print
The Gondola
In the Hammock
Last Dive
The Museum
Watering Horses
Sun Figure
The Comfort of the King

To Isabel

I

THE PARROT

Thinking in terms of how to solve worldwide malaise,
I watched the parrot in his cage, an old imperialist,
Perched on the swing that goes East and West, languorously
   dividing his predatory ways.

Kept in the kitchen, he remains a mandarin, a Sung,
Proud and dynastic, petulant to servants,
Speaking always in the slightly unreal accent of a foreign
   tongue.

He makes you think of opulence and squalor all together,
Messy with his food, impossible to please,
Arthritically rigid if too many he despises forgather.

Whether you were closed in your drawing room or free outside,
Alone, in the most raucous or diplomatic company,
You would be shaken if informed that he had died.

And why? Because he did not ever fully speak his mind,
Mocking, malapert, and just plain menacing the whole day long
Until he had no right, in death, to be so bland?—

A thing, if you were morbid, you might stuff
To remind you of the worldliness of crime
And how he made you wonder if you had lied enough.

THE SHOPPING CENTER

The girls with stark white faces and long hair
Heavy as grapes come to the shopping center.
They are idolatrous by nature and dream
Of golden bulls and motorcycles.
The boys come to the plaza in a gang,
Flash their cruel smiles and loiter.
The stores are loaded with aging patients,
Carts outside gleam like aids for paraplegics,
Abandoned women trundle meat-shop babies—
There is no other anatomical display.
If only there were an orchard near
Where one could hear the fall of peaches,
If only the boys could fondle warm plums
In the sun. If there were a fountain,
Supported by satyrs metamorphosing,

Some girl would sacrifice herself and stand
Naked there, bovine, marbling round
A root of flesh. In the shopping center
The troops have always only just moved through:
There are only and always grown-up urchins
Wanting someone to figure himself alive,
Stand in an arabesque of plums and pears,
Shining with a light that totally regilds.
There is a fatigue so abject in the plaza
That every demolition expert has his way.
The girls with their grape-hung hair, the boys,
Classic in such unexpelled desire,
Grow heavy, static, as nothing changes,
And the man in the last car that takes
A savage turn around the ruins reports
The situation there is well in hand.

THE PARURE

Passing the automobile graveyard, I saw one
Like one I owned—a defunct jewel of motion—
Nevertheless, it blinded me for a moment in the sun.

The green jewel-tones were foolishly, thrillingly, alive again,
And I knew that part of that hoard belonged to me,
A figure on the totem-mass of grandiloquent, yet garish, human
    stain.

It was like a quick look in a tinted mirror—
How had a part of myself become encrusted and embedded
In such public passions that were an aggregate of terror?

I was moving along the road in my own place,
A sunny little prince of subtly deliquescent life
Who felt so hard and gem-like strung upon that shining
    necklace.

Yet there it gleamed instead of Yorick's skull—
I step on the gas as quickly as I can and speed
To where the hill is once more soft and beautiful.

But it lurks in dreams somehow, a faulty helmet or a crushed
    green chalice:
Motion seems both random and meticulous,
And a crazy old king rides in the car, heavy with malice.

CHORES

The sea can make the way we keep our houses seem
Dirty, noisome, impossibly cluttered.
We should take the heart out, as though it mattered,
And see if the waves can wash it clean of slime.

Hardly, when feeling clings so limpet-like,
Medusa's head too subtly buried there—
How can we rush about and broom the floor,
Uncertain when the writhing cramps will strike?

Still, the sea, great energizer, laps
At the threshold, foaming like a soapy pail
Which knows our living has grown stale
And needs a scrub with something more than hoarded slops.

No doubt, a lucid morning, Neptune-disinfected.
But the heart that once turned Perseus back
Resists the sea in total lack
Of tutelary gods who want their art openly inspected.

THE TREE-FROG

I was kept awake nearly all night by the tree-frog
Which provoked a nostalgia almost too keen to bear:
It had something to do with revolution and the underdog.

A sound so insistent is very like the rebel
Who tries to conquer us by sheer compulsion:
The complaint of the put-upon has something similar to tell.

I have a powerful nature in pursuit of pleasure,
Peace, good will, and I do not share
My time's contempt for passion balanced by strict measure.

And yet this aggression which is comparable to pain
Puts a cutting-edge on things, no doubt about it,
Making passion and balance themselves seem suspect or inane.

The brutal thing about our life, in its broad sweep,
Is that these urgencies are ubiquitous and constant—
Another night the tree-frog will still be there, and I shall sleep.

But if I play with form and feeling, I am also played upon—
The tree-frog draws a bow across my nerves,
And I am raw with harsh and heartfelt music just before dawn.

WITH THE SHOCK TROOPS

He is wounded, he cannot rise from the beach—
The entire sea is merely the wash of his blood:
Nothing reminds him of life but a choice of skulls in easy reach.

Any one of them could have capped the life he might have
  lived,
Some sodden with sand or festooned with brilliant bird feathers:
Out of the phantasmagoria nothing else was saved.

They roll in closer like a string of unmatched beads.
If mistaken for and hunted as a savage he must die,
Should he not be hung with the full array of primal needs—

Or at least his hand be pinioned with the choicest weight,
The brightly pebbled brain spilling from its cup,
So that it were known he had a stake in love or hate?

One life grossly lived but many fasted.
The mirage was fearful but wonderful indeed:
When he rises, he will not know how long the fever lasted—

Except at certain times a row of skulls will seem to sit upon
  a wave,
Little nests for things flamboyant or too large—
His wound, like a buried shell, will ache since it cannot rave.

REBUTTAL

Grave phrasing may not alter fate
But it can employ delaying tactics:
A statue set among roses,
A faun, perhaps, laughing, amorous.
As regards beauty, agnostics
Can never, never wait—
If they are straight, noses
Must be broken, testicles smashed.

                              Castrations, thus,

Are not the whim
Of one who felt a god in him.

Though, in the long run, all
May be litter and ephemeral,
Goethe said that beauty,
Like emeralds, heals.

If we are extraordinarily set
Against such spiritual sobriety,
Still there is something in the phrasing that appeals:
A pause, a blessing.
                                    Not quite, "Let
There be Light," but an old man turning
Language like the next most precious thing.

THE LAST PAGE BUT ONE

There will come a day when you will remember History all too
    well.
The deaths of kings and princes, shady politics at home,
Cleopatra and her asp and why the Bastille fell.

You will, for once, look the American eagle in the eyes,
And feel his vast, impersonal, amber stare
As though you cannot know too much and still be counted wise.

Somewhere, perhaps in sleep, you stroked the lion's mane
And sensed the heavy, heavy coursing blood of time
As it asserts its massive way through every sensual vein.

And you will ask yourself as you accelerate the brute intake
Of classic myths relived without a sense of form
If this could be by any chance the summer of the last
    heartbreak.

You will be bold enough to stand as on an autumn plain,
For autumn seems, in fact, to be the meat of History's mood,
And, in advance, relume the summer as one that will not come
    again.

In such a light the step beyond is calculated risk—
Awakening the lion, flushing the bird, keeping the angry doors
    wide open,
You never let the heart remind it is not equal to the task.

II

ON THE EDGE OF THE KNIFE

There is something to be said for Holofernes
Who was not so heavy with the guilt of power
He could not pause like a pendulum in his strength and take
    his ease.

In one sense, no doubt, a great, lusty, passionate fool
Who yet could see Judith as she could no longer see herself:
Widowhood, like disease, had made her beauty seem merely
    bleak or terrible.

There was the lounging male, stretched out, immense and
    whole—
When she cut off his head, her fingers streaming hair
Brought up the hugest catch of all out of the troubled waters
    of her soul.

Into the meat sack it went, the dark, shining gobbet, severed.
Perhaps you have lain awake at night and thought of his ghost
    wandering,
Or, struck down in love, tried to keep your headless state
    from being implacably discovered.

It is not, as you well know, heartless that the unloved go down
    to death
But wondering, as the heart sticks in the chest, what it was
    that they did wrong.
The head of Holofernes hung upon the wall, startled in its
    last breath

That meant to feed lust, perhaps go tender, make love thrive—
The eunuch found the body, bewildered where the passion went,
But Judith, who had trapped one end of it, lived to be a
    hundred and five.

SOME, NOT ALL

Women have loved bulls and swans,
God in the form of a golden shower.
Now machines stamp out both swan and bull
And one can shake an aura from a box.
But something in the meretricious present tense
May indeed protect the beautiful—
Those persistent dreamers and their swan necks
Will rut somehow and hide their power:
Mothers, lacking vows, get along on tricks.

I have known one or two who slept with God,
Caught them looking down along some pool,
Or drenched in sunlight's spiritual seed.
One who followed hoofprints in the mud
Seemed, of all, in purest need
And certainly, to me, not cynical.
They would have thought themselves depraved
To pose as innocent or fool
And never once ally themselves with what the body craved.

When it was over and done with, one said,
Sprinkled with gold, bruised and beaked,
I am an ordinary woman and would have stayed
So if I had not been harshly used.
The swan retreating, the bull running, thus
Took on the look of those who were refused.
She had no trouble trading sensual death
When Minos, Castor, Pollux, Perseus,
Would bulge and struggle in the womb of myth.

THE SAVAGE

With a passion for fictions, he became the form
Of the swimmer, diver-companion, lover of bathing girls—
That way, at least, he said, I cannot come to harm.

And the mind lived like an island in the pool,
One with its sleeping volcano that had not erupted in years,
Reflecting roses, full of haunts, progressively more floral.

All the cannibals were extinct, though they had eaten men.
And he could watch without lust all the divers,
Including the shadow-figure of himself, pose and dive again.

Then with a rumble the crater began to smoke,
Spew out fire, and turn the pool to molten lava—
In the last strip of blue a diver made one last, ecstatic stroke.

This is a crisis, he thought, not accidental nor unplanned.
And then, like a cannibal, he looked around to see
If all the positions in the water were now unmanned.

But they were there, as they had always been, diving in and
out.
Only the island had sunk in fire and the primitive survivor
Came up in fear to ask the brilliant images what country lay
about.

19

THE LEPIDOPTERIST

The lepidopterist in the muslin dress
Stands in thick leaves, caught in a sturdy net.
She does not know this, though the pressure is febrile.
She has been absolutely and forever located:
There is no need for anything so blatant as the sudden grasp.
But the reason she does not know this
Is the butterfly transfixed upon a bush.
It opens the forest for her, it leads
Her to believe she parts her power
As she moves. Those who took the butterfly
As symbol for the soul knew what they were about.
It never for a moment doubts the circumstance
In which it lives. Fluttering or immobile,
It tests the net or sucks its essence,
Waits for the huntress living down the years
To find it in some mended, pulsing part,
Align it, a possession that has strayed.
The brusque command goes out: Come home.
And indeed it comes not unwillingly in death.
The world seems much less static, even free,
Lustrously the forest folds into itself,
And the beautiful relaxed girl goes home,
Herself a wing-like blur across the fields,
Armed with a perfect specimen to keep
From having to forever count on dreaming.

ON THE FRINGE

The woodchuck runs in his fat like a shrunken, exiled Eskimo.
I am the Sun to him, a bronzed, metallic enemy,
The tall god who melted down his world of snow.

Waddling on all fours, he searches for the merest trace
Of those foundation blocks which held his dome of ice—
Nothing could be more eloquent of what we mean by losing
    face.

On the run he has the look of never catching up
With that last whiff of arctic air, the glacial footstep just
    erased,
The sound of the self-annihilating igloo's dripping top.

What speaks displacement more than burrows in the ground?—
I was indeed the Wyrd, my face much larger than his shelter's
    mouth,
Peering down upon the desperate compensation I had found.

With an influx of air from Canada, the day reversed—
I could figure in my dreams an icy skull upon a pole
And was not in myself so fulsomely immersed.

All told, it had not yet come about, the woodchuck's day.
He must suffer in his little parka, pathetic refugee,
Understanding, with some malice, the changeling image of
    the stray.

OCTOBER

The effects of the furnace are there
Though the heat itself has cooled.
Make no mistake, no one was fooled:
Something was being fired in the summer air.

The work was mainly in pure gold
Until someone went passionate with color
And claimed vermeil was in order
If the full story of fire were told.

A whole landscape looks like the work of smiths
Who knew just how to turn the days
According to one cabalistic phrase
Which might suffice for all our personal myths.

No one, therefore, is utterly estranged in autumn
And yet no one feels too much at ease.
The gunshot, a gust of wind, can make us freeze
As though we guard these things of fire from sudden doom.

THE TURKEY

I have not known enough, perhaps, of dove or nightingale
But the turkey is aboriginal of my country,
Hiding an Indian's head in his broad tail.

Unwieldy, thus, he hoards the sanguine past—
With hood and neck of a scalded serpent,
He guards raw meat, his body like a murderer's chest.

It seems the best of luck that he is grounded
For a whole story might fall from his wings
And the air rain flints or tomahawks impounded.

When the wind catches his fan, the ghost of a scout
Wavers uneasily under a ruffled war-bonnet,
Trapped on earth too low for any last look-out.

So the bird I know is like a gaudy catafalque.
If you should carry a secret hump upon your back,
You, too, would have a burdened and uncertain walk.

This is what it is to spread an image in the sun—
This is how we teach thick, precarious balance as if the land
    moved like a ship
And one set sail heavily, slowly, encumbered with imagination.

III

THE FISH OBSERVED

He gasps in the sand before the still life in him wins,
Fighting the effect, fighting the cause as well, for that matter:
If he doesn't become a painting, he may end up in tins.

He is the spokesman for those who would not be arranged.
He made the mistake of rising to the bait, the dream of plenty,
And felt remorse hemorrhage through his hooked head—an
    undersea Utopia expunged.

Panting, streaming blood, mythical as a heart,
He has the totally denuding experience of being pitilessly
    observed
And a glaze comes into his eyes like milk glass buttons on a
    sequined shirt.

All blue and silver shadow jellied in the plate, sliced lemon,
    and a knife—
The saving grace is that these dead pieces may be strangely
    beautiful:
What sang back and forth along the line if it were not
    postulates in strife?

There is penitence in the look of the scarred but loving eye
Which has itself hung more than once upon a hook,
Observed how little it could do and what it might blindly try.

Will we not always, then, detect a covert spasm
In the thing accounted for, ruthlessly secured, the cut-and-
    dried,
As if the eye supplies the garden of the sea for this uncovered
    rhizome?

SKIN DIVER

The poet of the body seldom likes the night
Enough, prefers the day for making love—
Caressive Anti-Eros wears a rubber glove,
Concerned his operation will go right.

And yet these men, *au fond*, are twins—
We often hear love's other side is hate—
It seems suspect that dark can aggravate
The one and light remind the other of his mortal sins.

While Eros feels the whole day through alive,
His brother hangs his darker suit along the hall,
Lies naked in his room and shudders at the fall
Of figures in his dreams as they succinctly dive.

But in the dusk his own flesh, phosphorescent, glimmers
As though he, too, with vestiges of light were struck.
He rubbers up, a prowler born, regretful of his luck,
Prepared, abruptly surfacing, to spread panic among the
swimmers.

THE BEACH

The water looked like a liquid poured from the mind in its
bluest hour.
Now it had its own vast skin full of embolisms,
And it needed the conscience of the sand which was white as
flour.

There it was, portentous, lewd—objectified.
Its sliding back and forth was perilous, hysterical
As someone talking on hour after hour about some great pride.

One felt curiously calm, mindless then, glad that it was there.
One could see all of its bruises, lumpish arrogance,
Feeling some relief when suddenly the integument would tear.

Then all around us the blue blood of thought—
We are like plaster figures whose feet are stained,
Having trampled our secret share of grapes that come to naught.

One would like it to be precise, like bluing in a cup, more
positive, less loose—
By our white gestures it should be brought to heel
As one strangles—almost but not quite—a bluebell in a noose.

And yet the giddy plaster figure feels quite bowled over—
He is borne down and under in blue raiment, a discarded saint,
Or given a fish like a knife to mutilate the disappointed lover.

THE CONSUL

When the Consul got to his post, he found
The name of the country had misled him
And he wished he had been sent as a spy.
Though the rich women were festooned like birds
And the men wore spats and their monocles
Fell out like clear coins from a slot machine,
It was impossible to present his credentials.
The man who was the dictator could not
Be reached, and yet his odor streaked the city.
The police in their green uniforms splotched
The streets with a fungus of his power.
A motorcade met the Consul like a snake

As if it would play at Cinderella
With his fate, leading the black limousine,
Swerving through the plazas toward the palace
Before it turned into a wriggling worm.
Luckily it was a city by the sea
And threw hard mirror-lights into the eyes
Or, when the sun was underneath the clouds,
Presented a fat, rumpled throw of silk
Assassins wiped their bloody knives upon—
It did not encourage reimbarcation.
The Consul, in any case, was there to stay.
The baroque apartment provided by his country,
Saturated with an old commission,
Prepared to change his motives for its own.
This was the country of his dreams, there was
No question of a transfer. He had served
Around the globe only to reach this land.
If he was not received by the wizened gnome
Decked out in full regalia, he was lost.
No wonder, passing the palace, he felt
Sideswiped by a knowledge too close to tears.
But night was tender with its sorrow, he slept,
Awoke, and found the sunlight ribboned him
Into the world, pulling at his carcass
Like a gaudy cart, and nothing had changed.
There was no such thing as a retirement,
He must remain in contact with the land.
The Consul had been sent there for a purpose
But it was hard to remember just what it was.
Again that day he examined his emotions
Like a chemist holding up bright liquid
In clear tubes, and the colors barred the light.
Well, then, he was a representative.
Just that. He was there for saturation.
The festival of brilliant bird-women,
The men with monocles, relied upon
The stranger who had come to counsel them
Or conjure them from secret alchemies.

THE VENDETTA

So they had beaten him, kicked him in the groin,
    left him like a bleeding, golden rag upon the beach.
    They had wanted to use him to erase an icon,

The illumination he made upon a brilliant day:
    white sand, blue-green water, the bluer sky,
    needed just this burning image to have a final thing to say.

For it was almost in the sense of completing a mosaic
  he had wanted to insert his vital touch of form
  to show the world that he could make it stick.

Experience was in no way limited by the forceful scene:
  The sea raged on either side, the blue ejaculated its lightning,
  but with his gold he could impose something almost Byzan-
    tine.

They saw his purpose and they meant to blot it out—
  There would be a stark hole, a pure nothingness, where he
    stood,
  and they could take ship on the very void which they made
    float.

But the crumpled stuff itself cried out to the sea
  which rumbled in, insane with cure and grief,
    and stretched itself flat as a canvas where the gold cross
      might be.

VOYEUR

He undressed beside the sunlit pool,
Stripped at last like an Indian who survived
The racial wars, a secret that had thrived
Somehow, still watched by the water's winking jewel.

We, too, are watched, go through his motions with him—
The nude in us is forever furtive
Yet seeking every chance to live,
Granting that the great eye never will go dim.

It must happen and yet be truly seen:
This is what we ask for others and ourselves—
Now the clandestine diver in us delves,
And, like a sick eye, the water loses what we mean.

There is nothing to do but come up streaming anguish,
Scrape ourselves like Indians until we gleam
With some hard, joyous burnish of a dream
Men have, lucid-risen from an eye that does not languish.

THE LOBSTER

One thinks of beautiful women with violet eyes, champagne,
Despite the fact the restaurant window is a sordid peepshow
Where the beetle-like creature prowls, torpid and insane.

One remembers the music of violins plucking at a sexual nerve
As those antennae reach blearily toward us through the glass,
Provoked by some right of intimacy to do more than just
  observe.

We are nacreous to each other, we will not find one pebbled
  fault
To make the pearl for some lissom, dark-skinned diver—
Yet the little grotto-world groans of the sea, its weed and salt.

We must have the whole coast blue as blue can be
With white-sailed days and sequined nights,
And never smell, as the wave breathes out, the underarm of sea.

Romance is manic when it glows and glimmers in the street—
The lobster makes a move as though to present lovers to each
  other,
Our wriggling forms held in opposing claws like sweet, white
  meat.

We have been thrown into the other's arms and we embrace
Shamelessly now while people pass in sunlight murky as an
  aquarium—
The lobster peers, as though through blinds drawn down,
  into a cold, familiar place.

POOL AT NIGHT

The eye is all blue iris and clear
As untroubled conscience or unquestioned right;
Since there is no pupil to deploy or pinpoint sight,
The huge darkness reveals nothing at all to fear.

Have you not wanted, thus, to enter another's eye
As though someone did not have the troubles that you hide,
Or think you do, until your flashing eyes deride
Another who cannot be your clarity of sky?

But, here, the pool is like an enormous friend,
Half-sleeping, who gives you his divided but unmoted stare
As though he half-way knew you are and are not there
And do not need two eyes until you blend.

At that exquisite moment when you dive—
Sun-brown, ruptured from your shadow-brother—
Suddenly, no iris and all pupil, the other
Eye converges on the force and fate of man alive.

IV

SCHOOLING THE WALRUS

Making the world over, one comes upon a danger sign.
The walrus, who manages to look both fat and wizened, will
    not move over—
He has been obdurate since that day he pushed his face
    into a porcupine.

He will not move over in your expansive dream,
He must be fed oysters unless you expect to kill him,
Unless you are prepared to go to some inexorable extreme.

Otherwise, there is nothing left but ingenuity and technique:
Try to turn those flippers into cushioned wheels and let the
    slow poke ride
Unless you are ready to immolate and let him burn for a week.

Back to actual cases since he would not make an omnibus:
You will have learned to crowd, to be brutal and yet kind,
If you can persuade him he never was, and never will be, what
    was known as walrus.

But take care, trying to remove those quills of sorrow on his
    face,
The Neanderthal wrinkles, the tusks like stalactites of drool:
Mutatis mutandis—It is far better to revise and not erase.

Making the world over, one must save up monstrous parts—
Part whale, part mutilated horse, a roadblock on your way,
The walrus *is*. You feed him oysters, embrocate your dream,
    the damage done in fits and starts.

THE MISTRESS

Where, indeed, is the nest of love? The place
Of silk and satin will not do—It fades
And tears, recedes into the Aubusson.
The naked feet, deep in plush, leave no traces
For the archeologist. Where is the *gîte*
Of love? One feels the pillows shift and part,
The adorable, soft body threatens
To give at the seams and one cannot hang
In that sling for more than a purling moment.
The seedy room and the dirty bedclothes
Will not do—It is nuzzling and stroking,
Talking endlessly as if one laid down
The psyche's twigs to make a jackstraw bed.

He remembers her as having titian hair
Curled in a letter like a copperhead,
He remembers her as being violet
And dark, tented like an Arab, her hair
Heavy on the humps of her white shoulders.
"I want you darling. I am ever yours."—
The phoenix flies in like a carrier:
Somewhere, somewhere, is all that he can say.
Meadows flame across the shattered exit,
The future opens like an amorous mouth.
He listens to the waterfall she breathes,
And rows like a naked savage underneath its spray.
One element at a time, she will subsume
Earth, air, fire—"I want you, darling. I am
Yours forever." No other place will do,
Twig upon twig, branch upon dropping branch,
As if one could not lie down any other way,
Sleeping on the body as though it were an egg
That would revenge us for the meager world.

THE SIAMESE TWINS

When one is wildly alert, suppurating images,
The other wants to doze, be reclusive, retain himself,
But his brother, that unbalanced performer, lets all the animals
   from their cages.

Then, like a tide, the energy that belongs to Eros takes
   another tack.
He wants to eat, drink, voraciously make love,
But there, like an intolerable burden, is that dead animal on
   his back.

He would like to rest in the dark of the room and not be
   singed,
But brother wants the fire, glowing, burning there
Like meat on a stalled spit to which his flesh is hinged.

Yet, his thoughts pulled like elastic, disparate, forced, he feels
   too gelid and remote,
Requires the fire, wants to thaw and drip his juices there—
What, if he is not given place, can he do but grip his brother
   by the throat?

If one is continent, has the other sinned?—
If he stays healthy, will some bleak infection spread
Because one is irrevocably and forever to that gross traveller
   twinned?

INVENTORY AT AN AUTUMN WINDOW

Did we spend the summer on the essential?—
Then why is the sky so full of falling profit?
Are we serious, like the world situation, or caught in marginal
    regret?
Should one dip into grief perhaps as into capital?

Agreed at least that something else might have been better
    done:
Still one remembers ripe fruit, women, tennis, sweat.
Oils did ooze, our hands are fragrant yet
With so much bloom wiped off and so much sheen.

We have indeed the smell of life upon our fingers.
The question mark itself is light as feather
In this slightly musk and gold-leaf sort of weather—
Do we not rise from every mistress with our languors?

The daily truths of living accumulate their waste—
Let us be glad that here our premises can fall
In gestures, for the most part so symbolical,
That say, even essentials have their aftertaste.

Certainly there is a sense of powers overturned,
A hint of fire and golden flak of war,
But emotions, too, still bathe us in their shower—
In such slow-motion we survive what we have learned.

V

THE POSSIBLE DREAMS OF SWANS

Who knows but the swan may dream
Of being some one other,
To the hippopotamus a brother,
A water-thug enamored of a crime?

Nature scatters forms like pollen
And then the dreaming grows and turns:
The fecund, formal, bird-nymph yearns
For singed jowls and belly grossly swollen.

And yet it never comes to harm,
Stays beautiful, a white flute
Rising from the passions of a brute
Because it does no more than test its form.

Ah swan, the lake is easy with you now
Because you tempted it with waves,
A dark ship bellied out with slaves
Spilling pink-gummed from the horny prow.

THE CLOWN

Say that the clown became more broken-hearted
Than he should and yet held on until the laughter ended—
To the happiest man self-righteously departed

The best things and the right thing can happen now:
He leaves his victim mangled in the tent,
His emotions do not need that figurehead upon their prow.

The great white light, the open sea, lie full ahead.
How good it is to leave the working-shop of laughter
To one so versed in what it is to be deserted.

And yet the voyage keeps harking to the nest
His body makes, like a ship that dreads its skeleton
Lying somewhere breached upon the Islands of the Blest.

We would go back to the clown if we were bolder
Before he quite unravels his blood-buttons to the bone
And, shy as a nascent Pierrot, peer from his shoulder,

Figure our love, a little prow in his behalf,
Whispering, as he lies dying and exhausted there,
Our sailor's chastened joy if he would rise and make us laugh.

THE GALLERY

The dark, elegant woman walked in the gallery
And forbade the paintings to assault her,
The men with pointed beards, the wild peasants, the acrobats.
Ugh! But they were handsome, oppressively rough, lethal.
All leered for assignation, all a secret brotherhood.
Why should a woman be only flesh to them,
A clothed pod waiting for their burning seed?
Nevertheless it may have been significant
That she had had her portrait painted
And placed among them, and the artist,
Who was a man, had not seen her captive,
Rather, in his fantasy, as a gleaming Joan of Arc,
All modern-armored in her sequined dress—
Then why did she feel more naked than Venus?
First the bearded man, the peasant boy, and then the acrobat
Fondled her and found the secret target—
One day let them discover her dead
At the foot of her portrait, peeled out of it,
Viridescent as the Medusa, an enfabled octopus,
The rank, obscene thing a woman really was.
And the attempt at fornication would be over,
A beautiful, silent, unaggressive life
As among things that have weathered and weathered
Would dwell there, open to the public,
A presence that they would know as peace.

THE GOOSE

It will not do, it will not do, to say you are a giver
Of life, a life-enhancer, if you expect undue return
Like the man force-feeding the goose to fatten up his liver.

Clutched like a wine skin with a curious beaked spout,
The goose submits, rapt with ecstasy, abuse, his wide eye
    staring like a drop of wine,
Insane to know how food in such an orgy came about.

The man is very powerful, very efficient with his funneled
    grinder.
One must reach well down into the gullet to avoid choking
    or regurgitation—
If the eye is bloodshot, well, that may serve the goose as
    blinder.

It does not matter, if you are that force-feeder, what you say:
The goose is mindless, does not know if you are good or bad—
You give him his loathsome debauch to yield the best paté.

Which one of us has not been throttled for his good,
The common good, and waddled, bruised, stupified, away,
Feeling giddy yet beheaded, all bottom like a glutted sack,
    burdened and misunderstood?

I am told the goose will find a way out in disease,
Posing a morbid but authentic answer on a cracker—
It will not do, it will not do, to say you aim to please.

THE MIDGET

He stood between the women and their skirts
Parted like mismatched theater curtains
Merely to let him through. Thus he was ushered
Out of their inclosing world, their giant
Perfume pervasive as a forest all in bloom.
"I am the Little Prince. I am the one you love,"
He said, and indeed he was, their great pink hands
Fondling him like an octopus. And so the play
Would have to be enacted. Nothing but hands, hands,
Or breasts, breasts, lips, lips, one part at a time—
These ogresses dressed in magnifiers
Would never let him pause for as long
As it took to fall in love. When he bit their ears,
They screamed with pleasure and tossed him
From the earthquake of their breasts.
How could he love except by fetishes?—
This one gave him hair, that one, eyes, teeth,
The sweet, sweet bog of her plump navel.
They would stay wealthy all their lives.
Ten midgets would not make a man
Who robbed them in one seizure of desire.
All he could do was stand beside the bed,
Step shank-deep in that rank brutal shoe
And hobble round the fury and the sighs.
The discarded silks, the stockings, and the rings
Would tell him that someone had unified the world.

THE GIGGLER

There is, someone said and he laughed, a giggler abroad.
Women in their rooms alone hear him in the street below,
Reach for something at their throats as if it were a nylon
    stocking clawed.

The bride hears him titter when the groom puts on the ring,
The glowing athlete when he slips and flubs his vault:
The prima donna, hearing, almost forgets an aria she planned
to sing.

We choose, reflect, discard, reduce by half,
We move deeper into the shadow of our lives,
Accompanied always, it would seem, by that demented little
laugh.

You see you always leave your tracks in any part of town,
You do not know it but you move, constantly disrobe—
You are ubiquitous. You have no idea how ludicrous you look,
coifed or straggling down.

Oh, it is ambrosial to see a human being try
To love, to show his skill, recoup a loss, desperately endeavor—
Oh, I am going to laugh even if it kills me. Go on. Punch me
in the eye.

The giggler, he said and laughed, has such disaster to embrace.
Oh, oh, don't pull away—it breaks me up to see you play so
deaf, so dumb—
No need to hide, no good to lock your door. You'll see me in
the mirror, fingering the noose.

SKIN TALES

The tattooed thing swims in a life,
Detached, it goes wandering in the mind:
Anchors, Eagles, Snakes, and Venuses—rife
With places, passions, that we leave behind.
Did this come from arm, chest, belly, thigh?
What are we floating toward, by what held back,
Like blind men flashing on their hands a Seeing Eye?—
The Man with the Needle doubtless knows.
He tells us what our bodies lack,
Affixes it, and helps us button up our clothes.
Look how that rose gleams right above the navel—
Nothing matters but the vivid particle—
And now our dissolution seems the only way we travel
As though the sailor's unknown land were everybody's goal.
Is this unease only the wish to trade
Our permanences, our tattooes, with a friend?
Old tars whose hairy forearms do not fade
Have better notions of their journey's end—
They sit in the sun and reel their wanderings in:

The Eagle was a Swan, and Venus in her Shell,
The buxom tart who shimmied on his skin,
Is mild as mother, with nothing left to tell.

THE IMPERSONATOR

Was it a man impersonating a woman
Or a woman who had been impersonating
A man? One is here to be entertained—
She comes forward rich as smörgåsbord,
Wearing a voluminous iridescent dress,
Jewels heavy enough to weight the tented figure,
Nomadic, alone, an anti-climax
To those who come to see what they already
Think they know. She is a door ajar
Into the dressing room where we see him
Wriggling into the sheath like an erotic fish,
His feet spread in the flippers of a tail.
Thickly made up and smeared with ambergris,
The gill-hair of false eyelashes attached,
He pulls on long gray gloves smooth as eel skins.
Then the massive touch is in the wig
Which draws her up onto the dry land
Of speculation. Do not be deceived.
She gives them what they want but then not really.
Being born in a thousand wanton minds
Is not so easy. They nudge and snigger,
Yet there is something uneasily pneumatic,
They are willing to admit, as if they
Helped prepare a figure on parade,
Knowing a man was sewn in by mistake.
Someone in there is breathing his own air.
The breasts look out like enormous eyeglasses,
The sealed armpits agonize to sprout with hair.
When she takes off the wig, his head fumes up,
Made of solid gas. The women gasp,
But then there is nothing to do but laugh
And laugh as if to break some windows
In a place too thickly pressurized;
They clap and flap like a weakened fabric—
Backstage, the man is soon deciduous,
Resigned and fatal as an autumn tree.

VI

THE CAMEL

Ah, yes, we have come upon soulless, bitter lands—
It is a place for the desert pirate in blood-stained burnoose
With slave girls as the only spangled weight to murderous,
    wandering bands.

Yes, we have come, as if by instinct, in blood and milk
    ambivalently clad—
The cruel, ironic glance of the shaggy-lipped camel
Greets this devastating horde, this ultimate nomad.

Oh, yes, there will be, under clear stars, the musk of an
    embrace,
Reaching into the captive body as toward a last oasis,
Hearing the bracelets clank, the veils torn to show the belly
    like a vacuous face.

All this mingled with the smell of camel's urine, camel's dung:
Nothing could have carried us here but an animal which looks
    like a cutthroat
Who would lap up the last liquid of blood with his thick,
    black tongue.

There he stands, fringed round with ragged girls and boys,
Humped up, an odious but implacable dune of flesh,
As the bodies croon in the hot tents or ejaculate abuse.

I know him, you know him, we crouch on his saddle in an
    arid, bright room—
We made cutouts of him as exotic and wandering children,
We tether him nearby and give him the drouth of the heart
    for his violent home.

BIRD PRINT

Imagine flamingoes by the pool, flamboyant, intense,
One leg lifted, with stalking, almost predatory, look.
Listening, their necks in lethal crook,
They seek, lacking prey, an audience.

Or so it seems. And in your opulent rapture
You wonder if someone is looking, if someone is there
To give the slightest gesture that they care
How much you spend upon their capture.

Thus it is a static thing, almost a precious painting,
Except for the brazen way you made it be at all:
Choked blue, hot pink, the suppressed call
For someone standing by to go into a fit of fainting.

One more step puts into the beak a thread
And motions to the world as labyrinthine—
Someone there and there until the thread engorges like a scene:
At last the heart of the flamingo, inward-reeled.

THE GONDOLA

Something remains, no matter how much may have been
undone.
Those who have never been to Venice may find that it supports
them—
A gondola floats along side like a beheaded, breached, black
swan.

One would not always be held accountable or pay too dear
For all that our dreams may seize upon,
Or make a Charon on the river Styx out of every gondolier.

Black, breached, beheaded, but it still moves!—
A whole city made of Turner's "tinted steam" may be outmoded,
But is this the way we want to judge our loves?

At rest, then, at rest, with a black swan on a leash—
Motorboats flash by in the moonlight, an abstract push,
and that too
Must teach us something more about living on pastiche.

The grasping imagination may not be altogether blind,
Hungering near the water and the darkened bridges
As if assignations with the *contessa* were variously assigned.

Let us indeed give our best images both room and air,
Fishing for the Doge's ring if that were our true salvage,
Putting a head upon the beheaded thing, providing the black
swan's stare.

IN THE HAMMOCK

Hung in the wind, a heavy, supple jewel,
All of a man, body and mind, is lumped together.
What makes him love crumples against what makes him cruel.

43

At least no bruises menace from the bag,
But this is a richly stuffed tranquillity:
The wind is gentle as it pushes at the dangers of that swag.

This is indeed the one who got away,
Having dined, no doubt, on wine and pheasant
And put his senses through their paces as on a final day.

His hand hangs down in languor like a fuse—
Not long before, it may have stroked and then let go
The one who went to any lengths to be the victim that he
  chose.

Not one of us who come upon him really mock
This tranquil, blooded, jeweled man,
A sensual king not counting on the sudden shock

Of someone rude enough to cut him down—
We even wish him silk instead of canvas for his bed
As summer whispers its most mortal song across the placid
  town.

LAST DIVE

The mat of the diving board is worn
With Mercury's heels. He took off here,
And fell into the pool, a god's blue tear—
We sag, we sag, the world feels torn.

Autumn leaves are blowing from the side
Of summer as though it hardly mattered
Whether things are broken, merely scattered,
Or if the wound were local or world-wide.

I do say this, however. I am not among the totally nonplussed.
The soaring glimpse was right, the fall,
As well, was hardly hypothetical—
Emotions do not get too far when they are trussed

Too tight, and count their riches, playing safe.
I search the board for spikes that go with wings—
I saw him shoot toward his shadow-underpinnings
As though the sun could not detain him nor the brisk air chafe.

THE MUSEUM

So many brilliant and defeated lives were there
It was almost like bright, bedraggled birds cawing at each other
Until the aviary was thunderous with ecstasy, despair.

No wonder the guard frowned on any personal noise.
Something in common with a bomb only superficially stable
Might easily have been ignited by one more human voice.

The tension was filled with being, being, being—
Back into the history of all the birds—the snake,
And the laborious ascent into the trees for better seeing.

We fed this one and that one but then a beak
Nailed in the frame like the headdress of a savage
Reached out, as we passed by, and left a scar on hand
    and cheek.

Would it have been better to come in armor,
Knowing how pigeons foul the statues in the square,
And move with reptilian eye mercilessly among the clamor?

No, this would have been going back too far in time and place.
We must provide somehow a living stem, a Babylonian tree,
Where birds can perch, secure, as on an artifact of peace.

WATERING HORSES

Seeing them drink, one wishes one were water
To be taken into rapt, deep-seated thirst:
It has never seemed such an important matter
For desire to be up to itself and yet not burst.
The water, if it could feel, should take great pride
That it gave fully of itself and satisfied.

To fill out the wish of some great beast,
 The horse at best, the hippopotamus at least—
To be fluid and yet thickly vital!
The big red belly yearns and yearns
As if it spent the day looking for requital
Of the way stone bruises and the wind burns.

The world suddenly stays utterly quiet around
The water and the powerful drinking horse.
Ecstasy has no more essential sound

And looms like a goddess who taught these forces to rehearse—
This threesome, and nothing, nothing at all
Can make life's drama picayune, ephemeral.

Once the horse has fully drunk, the world moves
Elsewhere in pursuit of other loves,
Lies slack or guards an unformed foetus,
Solidly sure at least of two well-met,
The slaked horse and the water in quietus—
No accusations, no denials, and no regret.

SUN FIGURE

Like some mythological sun-toad with a human head,
He squats at the pool's edge, and one half expects
His mouth to spout water, but he erects
Himself and suddenly becomes a man instead.

Still golden, still glistening, but now much more cerebral,
The most superior ornament a fountain shows.
Now, if we look, the water of the spirit overflows
Down the sunny back of the toad, metamorphosed, yet inherent
   still.

Regard, however, the lucid, collapsible myth—
More than the fact that we are too much flesh or mind
Is the terror, joy, that strikes us blind
When we follow one without the other into its pith.

Are we less a thing of parts than strange montage?—
The little fellow, hunched and happy in grotesque,
Reaches up as though the sunlight held a mask
And, right before our eyes, comes radiantly of age.

THE COMFORT OF THE KING

When all of your senses are brought to bed
By violence and the larger issues of our time,
Is it altogether wrong, my friend, to think of playing dead?—

Not forever, but for the long, long moment of repose
When all the machines are quiet, the orators silent,
And the spiritual warrior in you may without contrition doze.

Surely the healing dreams with all your darker ones will
    intertwine.
We must sleep and sleep again with health until the very end—
Life summoned to a failing David the lovely concubine.

Those who had heard the power leap and tremble in his veins
Could see the giant-killer sleeping in him still.
Who is to say, in our exhaustion, what virile love affair remains?

The lovely hand, indeed, in any sort of noisome weather
May stroke the sensual pelt and make it glisten
And thighs, depleted, tingle with the thrill of that experienced
    feather.

Shall we not think at the darkest moment of our truth
The golden hand will move among our senses with more than
    sensual aim
And put into our strong, awakened fingers the slingshot wielded
    in our youth?